nF419415

Cuddy from the Beach

Written by
Angelina Rose Will

Illustrated by
Laura H. Torelli

To my number one guy, Cuddy. Thank you for anchoring me. Thank you for all the laughs, and thank you for all the adventures. Those who know, know. My OG.

What's a Cuddy?

Well, we're not sure, but he was found at a beach.

Which beach?

A beach way, way, way down in the Florida Keys.

You see, Cuddy was found roaming the shoreline.
He was following his nose to the scent of food.

Cuddy wound up under umbrellas with his head
bopping in and out of coolers.

He didn't belong to anyone, so we were never
told what he was.

What did Cuddy look like?

He had creamy colored hair with curls, which stuck to him in knots.

He had a smooshy, shaggy face with floppy ears, and two big brown spots under his big brown eyes.

Cuddy had four legs and a tail, which curled up.

He had little, crooked teeth, which came up out of his mouth over his lip and his itsy-bitsy tongue was sticking out.

Cuddy was a dog who looked like a fluffy, stuffed animal!

Where did Cuddy come from?

Maybe Cuddy belonged to a sailor who was lost at sea.

When a giant storm came, Cuddy had to swim ashore alone.

OR...

Maybe Cuddy wandered away from his family to chase after yummy food smells, before they lost him.
EEKLY

OR...

Maybe Cuddy's parents could no longer afford his fancy food habits, and dropped him off at one of the Keys best restaurants.

What happened to Cuddy?

After weeks of "beach bumming," someone asked animal control to come take him away.

Maybe because all Cuddy did was mooch for snacks. He was a "moochy-poochy."

Was Cuddy scared?

Animal control took Cuddy to his temporary home, the animal shelter, on Valentine's Day.

Everyone there realized Cuddy was so friendly, and never caged him.

Cuddy was a comedian, and loved playing with his cat friends.

Perhaps, Cuddy thought he was a cat!

How long was Cuddy at the shelter?

Cuddy was a very popular little doggy. Everyone seemed to want him.

Cuddy could finally be adopted after two weeks. A nice lady took him home.

She was nervous, since Cuddy would be her first dog, and wondered if Cuddy would like her. The lady knew she would love him with all of her heart.

What was Cuddy's new life?

Cuddy's new mom moved him further down the islands. There, he became used to a new life, filled with freedom.

Cuddy never wandered far from his new mom. He always listened when she called.

Some of his favorite things were playing in the sand and splashing in the water!

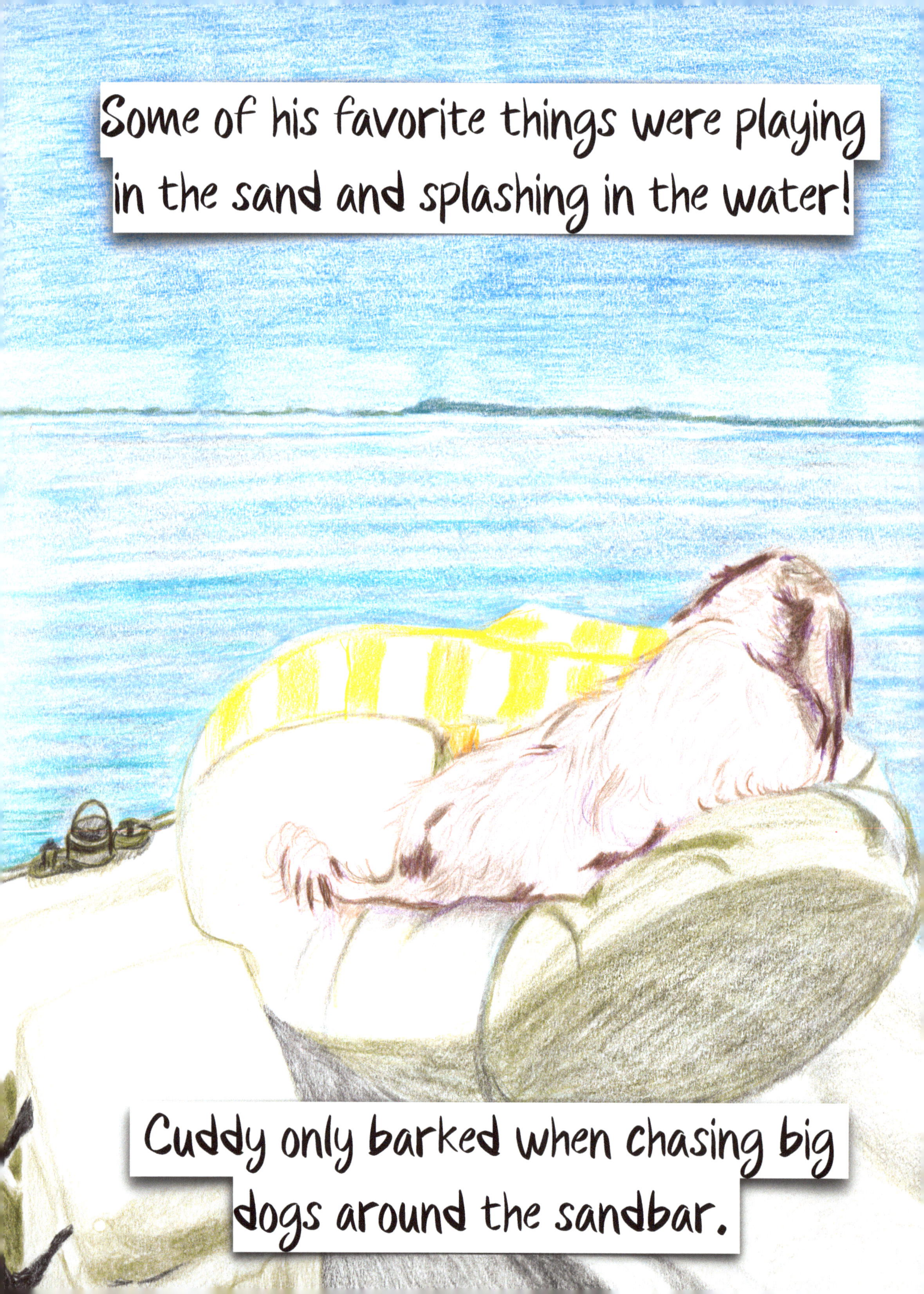

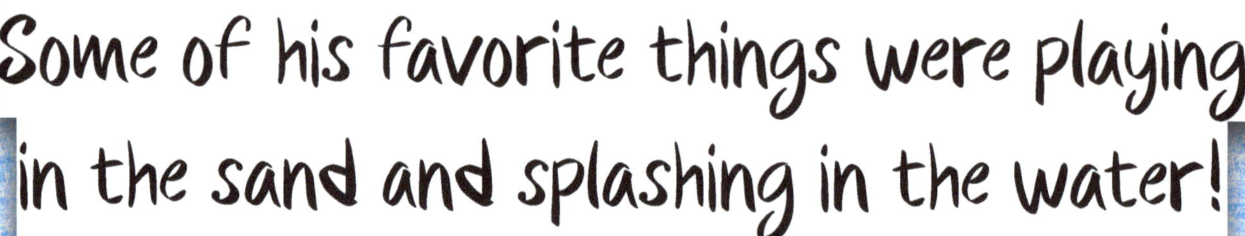

Cuddy only barked when chasing big dogs around the sandbar.

Did Cuddy like to travel?

Cuddy traveled to many states.

He lived in many houses with his mom, and even stayed on a boat!

Cuddy went boating and fishing all the time.

Cuddy was a special type of dog
who never lost his hair.

Cuddy also had a certain skin type, which
never caused anyone to sneeze or cry.

Cuddy didn't eat like a normal dog.
Cuddy was a foodie.

Cuddy had steak from the steakhouse,
fish caught by fisherman, and listened to
music at the tiki huts. Best of all, he had
a lick of fresh milk—milk
nightly at his moms.

Everyone in the Keys
loved Cuddy so much,
and always fed him the
best food and snacks.

EAD

Cuddy became a local celebrity. His new friends invited him to many parties! He loved parties!

Cuddy from the beach became "Conch Cuddy."

"Conch Cuddy" now says "goodnight" to his forever mom, from his forever home.

Angelina is a FL Keys based author, voiceover artist, and REALTOR®.

To follow Angelina's author and travel page check her out on Instagram:

@willfaring

You can also message her at:

angie@willfaring.com

Follow Cuddy on Instagram:

@conchcuddy